Colormazen

Easy Mandala And Mandala Patterns Book Volume 5

Carol Bell

Colormazen

Copyright © 2018 Carol Bell
All rights reserved.

This book or any portion thereof may not be reproduced or used in any manner whatsoever without the express written permission of the publisher.

ISBN-13: 978-1720428602

ISBN-10: 1720428603

DEDICATION

To my Grandchildren

Shannon, Liam, Grace, Stanley, Ollie, George, Émilie, Jake, Joseph and Jessica.

Coloring Instructions and Tips

This book may be colored using colored pencils, felt tipped pens, gel pens, markers, pastels and paints.

All designs in this book have been printed on the odd numbered pages.

The even pages have been left deliberately blank as some colouring mediums such as felt tip pens will bleed through onto the reverse side of the paper.

Always test markers or gel pens to check to see if it bleeds through or leaves a mark.

To make extra sure you do not get bleed through place a blank piece of thick paper or card behind the design that you are coloring and the next page.

We have made the designs in the early part of this book to be easy to color, for children or people with poor manual dexterity.

If you are an experienced colorist you could use shading or the blending of two colors to complete these simple designs.

Or use the space to expand the mandala or draw your own patterns.

Have fun and color outside the lines.

Happy Coloring!

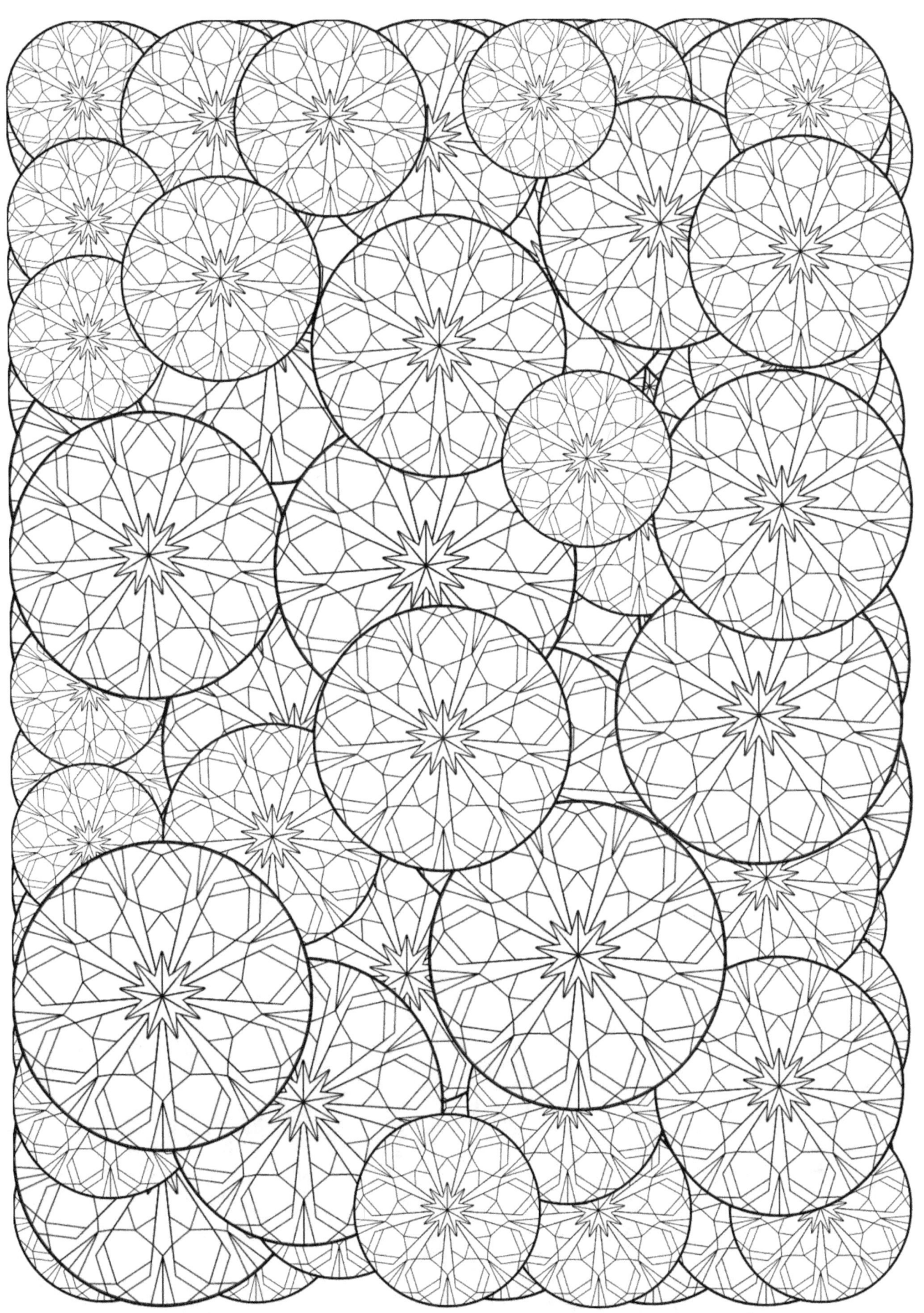

Final Words

If you have enjoyed this puzzle book and are interested in learning more about our other products and publications, please visit:

http://www.colormazen.com/

We design and write -

- Adult Coloring Books
- Mandala Coloring Books
- Pattern Coloring Books
- Sudoku Books
- Puzzle Books
- Crossword Puzzle Books
- Word Search Books
- Planners
- Journals
- Diaries
- Children's Books
- Children's Workbooks

www.ingramcontent.com/pod-product-compliance
Lightning Source LLC
Chambersburg PA
CBHW060002230526
45472CB00008B/1919